IDEA TO EXECUTION

The Ultimate 10 step Guide to Goal setting!!

IDEA TO EXECUTION

The Ultimate 10 step Guide to Goal setting!!

MANUJ ADLAKHA

Published Internationally by

Pendown Press

Powered by Gullybaba.com

PENDOWN PRESS

Powered by **Gullybaba Publishing House Pvt. Ltd.,**

An ISO 9001 & ISO 14001 Certified Co.,

Regd. Office: 2525/193, 1st Floor, Onkar Nagar-A, Tri Nagar, Delhi-110035

Ph.: 09350849407, 09312235086

E-mail: info@pendownpress.com

Branch Office: 1A/2A, 20, Hari Sadan, Ansari Road, Daryaganj, New Delhi-110002

Ph.: 011-45794768

Website: PendownPress.com

First Edition: 2020

Price:

ISBN: 978-93-90479-60-3

Layout and Cover Designed by Pendown Graphics Team

Printed and Bound in India by Thomson Press India Ltd.

CONTENT LIST

1

THE RE-UNION

After tying his shoelaces, Jayant got up to give a final glance at his look in the mirror.

"Perfect", He murmured.

Tonight, he was going to a very special reunion party. His old colleagues, friends, former bosses, all were coming to this party.

Hopping at the backseat of the car, he went bank in his memory lane.

In the past five years, he had toiled day in and day out to have his own identity in business. He had a clear vision about what he had to do and pursued his goal doggedly with love towards his work and unflinching faith that his hard work will bear fruit one day.

There were onslaught of criticism, brick bats, insinuation and discouraging comments. He was at the receiving end for leaving a secure job and go after ephemeral things. But, he was happy for himself today and he was thankful for that as, today he was a successful businessman.

The party was in full swing when Jayant arrived. One by one he met everyone. There was greeting, shaking hands, hugging and laughter followed by drinks.

Then came more serious discussions. Many of his friends opened their sordid saga—how they were bored to death in their current jobs, even their family life was not cordial. He also met Shekhar, his former boss who had grown old, bald and fat in these five years. Everyone almost had a similar thought process.

"I cannot take risks" "What is the need?"

"Higher profile means higher tensions, targets and travel... who wants that?"

"Then what do you want?" Jayant managed to ask one of his friends.

"I don't know, never thought about that" came the reply. "What? You don't know what you want in life?" Jayant was surprised.

Apparently his friend appeared to be more interested in food and drinks.

Jayant left them to enjoy their drinks

He bumped into Shekhar, after initial greetings Jayant could sense that Shekhar wanted to discuss something, so he took him to the nearby table.

When—they were seated Shekhar started complaining about his life. He had not taken any vacation for two years.

His family complained that he was too busy. He had no time for workouts which had resulted in his fat and aging posture. He was not satisfied or happy with his work-life. His wish to buy his favourite car had been laid on the back burner. All his enthusiasm was gone.

Shekhar was making a lot of effort to make himself audible but the party music was playing at the deafening level.

"Let us meet tomorrow for lunch at my office, we can discuss everything in detail", Jayant said, pressing Shekhar's hand.

THE MENTOR

It was one am in the morning when Jayant finally left the reunion party. As he sat back in his car; his mind recalled his meeting with his mentor 10 years back. Mr. Rajeshwaran-who was the director of a very big American IT company had given him a life transforming mantra that day as they sat down to talk, Jayant pictured himself as being in the same state of mind as he saw Shekhar today.

Jayant recalled how he described to his mentor about his childhood which had been full of struggles and unfulfilled desires. As a teenager he wanted a motorbike but he could not afford it. He was passionate about his career as a cricketer, but that didn't work out either. He wanted to set up a business early but due to financial constraints had to join a job instead.

In fact, he had many goals in his mind, but could never achieve them.

After listening to him for a while Mr. Rajeshwaran said," whatever has happened to you, is really the story of 97% people; I want you to share with me the list of your goals and we will see what is missing in that."

"What do you mean?"

"Just share the list of your goals" replied Mr. Rajeshwaran

"I don't have"

"I understand, go home and bring it tomorrow; it must be at your home or office or in some digital diary."

"I have never written it" was his reluctant reply.

Mr. Rajeshwaran looked at him with smile. After a pause, what he said next changed Jayant's life forever.

He said, "You have not written your goals, that is why you have not achieved your goals."

Jayant learnt a big lesson that day… Only written goals get accomplished!!

3 CHAPTER

WHAT IS SUCCESS?

Next day when Jayant met Shekhar at lunch, he was brimming with enthusiasm. He narrated the life transforming episode he had with his mentor a few years ago.

"Wow that is a great piece of advice, so written goals lead you to your success?" Shekhar asked.

"Now that we are no longer Boss and employee, can I take the liberty to ask you a question?" Jayant said.

"Yes, please go ahead and from now on you are my mentor" Shekhar smiled.

"What do you mean by the word success?"

"I believe that once you are rich enough to fulfill all your needs. You know… a nice car, a big house, lots of money, holidaying abroad…stuff like that." Shekhar said, moving his hands in air.

"Ok, it might be your definition of success"

"What do you mean by my definition of success? Everybody wants the same stuff, and then only he or she can be called successful. Shekhar emphasized.

"Ok, tell me how would you define a successful teacher?" Shekhar thought for few seconds and then replied," The one who is able to impart good education and values to his/her pupils."

"Ok and how can a housewife or a salesperson be successful?"

"A housewife can be called successful when she is able to raise a healthy family and give a good upbringing to her children. A salesperson can be successful when he is able to meet his targets and generate good business from his clients."

"Did any one of them have any similarity with your definition of success?"

"No"

"So it means what is success for you, may not be success for someone else and vice versa. You see success is subjective in nature. The word 'Success' has different meanings for different people."

"Okay…" Shekhar nodded.

"Earl Nightingale defined success in terms of goals in the year 1956. He said," "Success is really nothing more than the progressive realization of a worthy ideal. This means that any person who knows what they are doing and where they are going is a success. Any person with a goal towards which they are working is a successful person."

"Success is actually a journey, it is not a destination.

You keep

on setting goals

one by one

and keep

on attaining them.

That is success."

"I want to write it somewhere" Shekhar said, "So tell me what happened after that when your mentor gave you a new insight about goals?"

"It changed my life. I sat down to write my goals and how to achieve them. I quit my job in this company, I became a consultant for big multinationals; helping them in product launches and brand positioning. In the next two years I started my first company and then a second company after three years."

"But you need to have nerves of steel, risk taking capacity plus lots of funds to start a business venture...how do you manage those things?" Shekhar questioned.

"Actually Shekhar I went through many trainings, studied many successful people. I also had many mentors during this period of time. After all this I finally concluded that this one skill had played a very crucial role in every successful person's life...."

"What kind of skills?"

"There are some secrets which only 5% of people know

about. Those who know and apply them in their life are the top few successful people; the remaining 95% just follow them or work for them."

"Really? so, would you please unravel these mysteries?" Shekhar said imploringly.

Jayant smiled back.

INTRODUCTION TO GOAL SETTING

Shekhar would have loved to be with Jayant for the entire day but his wife called up to inform that his bag is packed and also requested him to come home because if he further delays, he might miss the flight. Shekhar was going from Delhi to Mumbai for four days.

After coming back from Mumbai, Shekhar again fixed up a meeting with Jayant.

"So, how was your trip to Mumbai?" Jayant asked.

"It was good. I attended a conference, did some shopping, met a close friend in Mumbai... everything went well." Shekhar replied.

"How everything went? Who looked after your work in your absence and how you managed to reach Mumbai on time, attend conferences, do shopping, and even meet your friend?"

"Oh, that was easy. I assigned my work to one of the team members. Pre-booked taxis and hotels, packed up everything I needed for the conference and during long lunch hour breaks I did some shopping, then, on the last day I scheduled my return flight at such a time when my friend was available for the meeting."

"So, you have unraveled the mystery yourself ", Jayant winked at him.

"What...what are you talking about?" Shekhar looked confused.

"That is the beauty of Goal setting. When we plan and execute everything to its minutest detail, we are headed for nothing but success."

"How can my travel to Mumbai be related to Goal setting? And what success are you talking about bro?" Shekhar emphasized "Let me get it straight to you. When you came to know about your trip, you planned everything in detail? You had specific goals. You set up a date for the journey. Then you pre- booked cabs according to your flight schedules. You booked a hotel; you made a checklist of all the things necessary for your stay in Mumbai for four days. Then, you assigned your work to someone. You even managed to find time for shopping and meeting an old friend. That is the finest example of goal setting in process." Jayant said in one breath.

"Wow, I never knew that I had such a skill," Shekhar said excitedly.

"Now, analyze its contrary part so that you could better understand the significance of goal setting. If you had not known as to when you had to visit Mumbai, for how many days you need to stay there, what would have been the mode of communication, from where you could have got a ticket or cab, etc., you would have remained at planning level itself. There would not have been execution, and even if there were execution at all, your journey could never be hassle free."

"That is so true. "Shekhar said nodding his head.

"Now, think about those areas in your life where you are not getting expected outcomes. You will see that the element of goal setting is missing there. That is the primary reason you are not succeeding in those areas... simple!"

"Yes, that is so true." Shekhar said in a pensive mood. "Now I realize the reason why I was failing at certain areas. I had no preparation at place to deal with them.

I had no idea how and when I was going to deal with them. There was no checklist. No specifics, no written goals for them."

"Now that you know how important this goal setting is; I will tell you what exactly the process of goal setting is."

"There is a process? Of goal setting? I thought I could just write them down on a paper." Shekhar said, picking up a sheet.

"Did you write that you had to meet your friend in Mumbai on a piece of paper? Or you called him up and fixed a meeting at a specific time and date?"

"I had to make sure that he was available for the meeting on that day, so I called him up before going to Mumbai. So, is this some kind of process? Shekhar asked.

"Yes, goal setting has a proper process. Only then, you can be sure of achieving those goals."

THE GOAL SETTING PROCESS

"The most crucial thing is to fix your goals." Jayant continued

"Yes, that is obvious..." Shekhar said.

"No, it is not. Often we have a wish in mind, but then something or someone influences us, and we want our life to be like that. We often get carried away by people and circumstances. This leads to continuous change of our goals."

"Can you elaborate it?"

"Suppose you have planted some seeds on a certain day. The very next day, or say after one week, a downpour occurs.

You lose some of the plants in this downpour. Do you drop the idea of plantation? Do you take out all the remaining plants cursing your fate? Or, you assess the loss, find its causes, and try to make yourself smarter with this incident and go for the remaining plants? In the same way, before fixing your goal, make proper permutation and combination, extensive research, and talk to the people you think will be important in this regard, but once you fix it, pursue it doggedly. So, know your goal, fix it and pursue it with an unwavering mind." Once you follow this process, your wish becomes your goal.

"But we are just human beings. When we see someone with a nice car, we want to have the same car. When we see someone wearing an expensive watch, we want that too...so, what is wrong in that wish?"

"There is a difference between a wish and a goal. I share my one goal setting process to help you understand. I once thought that I should double my profit. What you think? It's a goal or a wish? This will be termed as my wish (My mentor taught me this). Goals are realistic. My mentor then gave me this process. He said, "If I have to make it a realistic goal, then I need to specify as to how much profit will be made in specific time so that by the end of specific time my total amount will be the double of my current profit."

"Do these goals have any attributes?"

"Yes, every goal needs to have five attributes which will change it from a wish to a goal. You need to create SMART goals."

6

SMART GOALS

Jayant had an important training session for the next week, so he could not continue his conversation with Shekhar.

Shekhar too was caught up in his work, but the entire week he kept on thinking what SMART goals meant? There were smart phones, smart watches and even smart TVs these days; but what were smart goals?"

So when they finally met, Shekhar was eager to know about smart goals.

"For the entire week I kept on thinking about Smart goals. I only could come closer to the fact that the word was a kind of acrostic...each letter in this word means something... am I right?"

"You are a brilliant mind!! Yes, there is a particular meaning for each letter in this word. The first letter 'S' means that the goal should be specific. That means we must be talking in terms of numbers. Take my example, if I want to double my profit in the next six months, then I need to have a goal of a specific amount not just "Double the profit. "Numbers create magic. I must write the exact number—how much profit I want to generate for which month. Let us say, you will make a profit of 100k USD in the month of September. So, exact numbers make the goal more credible, sounds specific."

"Okay, I got that."

"The next letter is 'M' which stands for measurable. Once your numbers are defined, next you should set up a mechanism to track your progress. From the previous example, you can measure your progress after six months, or you can measure how much money you made in the first month, so that makes it measurable."

"Let me guess the meaning of the letter "A". Does it mean attainable?"

"Yes you are very close to that. It stands for achievable. Do you really believe that you can raise your profit, or you can double your profit in the next six months? It is important to ensure that your brain accepts it. If you write down certain numbers, but your brain shouts hey! That is impossible...how long you can go on denying that? It can also steal away your motivation and urge to achieve. So, it is very important that your brain accepts your goal as achievable."

"And the next two are...?"

"The letter 'R' stands for realistic. Now think about a seventy year old man who is very passionate about flying a plane. He wants to become a commercial pilot, even if he manages to get a degree in flying, will he get a license to fly? Certainly not; which means, that his goal is not realistic. In the example we are talking about, do you think that you can increase your profit in some extreme conditions such as lockdown, flood or natural disaster? No. So, before making any goals, think about your present scenario, and even do research wherever possible about the ecosystem."

Shekhar was in deep thought. Jayant continued...

"The letter "T" stands for time bound. We have made a perfectly time bound goal that we will increase our profit to 100k USD in the next six months. We are time bound to check our progress after three months or six months. So, if our goals are SMART then we have already won half the battle."

"Let me summarize again" Shekhar said. "S=Specific,

M=Measurable, A=achievable, R= Realistic,

T=Time bound. That makes it SMART."

WRITING YOUR GOALS

It was getting very late so Jayant dropped Shekhar at his home. As Shekhar was very eager to learn the rest part of goal setting, so they decided to spend the weekend in a nearby resort. They decided to leave at the crack of dawn to escape from the heat and traffic the next day.

After driving for about three hours, they stopped to have an early breakfast. Jayant continued his discussion.

"Now, we can get to the actual process of Goal setting. You see after thinking about the smart goals, you need to write them."

"That is obvious, as we discussed previously that written words are more powerful than verbal. "Shekhar recalled.

"Exactly, let me explain this with an example. There was a study in Harvard in 1979. It was the outgoing batch of 1979; they were asked two questions. Have you made goals? Have you written those goals? Only 3% of people replied that they had written goals and 14% of people said that they had made goals but it's in their mind. The remaining people had not even made goals.

After 10 years in 1989, all these people were tracked down. The results were very amazing: they could see that those 3% who had written goals, were far more successful than the remaining 97% people whereas these 14% people were more successful than those who had not even made goals, but they were far behind from those 3% who had written goals."

"Wow that is a real eye opener." Shekhar remarked.

"There is a very strong statement that 'only 3% of the people have written goals, and the rest of the world works for them'.

It is also very important that your goals should always be in front of your eyes. My goals are written everywhere. They are in my washroom, in my office; I have vision boards at my study room."

"Yes, but I have seen something written at your staff desks also... why? Are they your goals?"

"Yes, those goals which are related to my company are everywhere in my office. My accounts team, sales team, operations team knows what goals we strive to achieve. So, it becomes a common goal. It builds team spirit; it is no longer an employer or a company's goal. It then becomes everybody's goal. The moment you enter the office, you know exactly what to do to achieve your goals."

"So it is very important to write down your goals at a place where you and your team can read them every day."

"Yes, now let us move, and now I want you to drive." Jayant said giving car keys to Shekhar.

WHY AND HOW OF GOAL SETTING

They reached the resort in the next two hours. There was some time for lunch, so they decided to meet at the resort's restaurant for lunch.

"Let's take a short nap." Jayant suggested.

"Yes, I am badly in need of that." Shekhar said with a grin. Totally refreshed after a nap and a hearty lunch, they sat down at the lobby with their coffee mugs.

"The next step is to write down WHY you want to achieve these goals. It is like connecting your goals with a specific cause and adding to it an emotional factor."

"Sorry, I didn't get that... why do we need that, aren't your goals motivating enough?" Shekhar looked confused.

"There is a very strong statement which says, 'The louder your WHY is, the easier your HOW is'. This simply means that the more clarity you have on your WHY, that is: why you want to achieve a particular goal, the more easy it will get for you HOW to achieve them. Let me explain it with an example from my own life: My upbringing has been very tough in terms of financial aspects. We have gone through scarcity most of the time, and my relationship with money was not good. I was always in survival mode. I wanted to earn money only for survival, even after working hard, I earned only that much money which was sufficient for survival of my company. Then I attached an emotional aspect to my goal. I thought about my son. I always wanted that my son should not go through all that and that became my 'Why' to make more money. So, now this WHY drives me to earn a lot so that I can give a better life to my family and to my child. In the same way, you can have your own why and your why will drive you automatically."

"Okay, so that keeps you on your toes."

"Yes, most of the time it happens that people pull you down. They might sympathize with someone who has failed, but if anyone is working hard to be successful they will say why are you doing this? What is the need? Why are you not satisfied with whatever you have made till now? So the more challenges you take, the more upward you move in life, and the more you move upward, you will have less and less supporters. It's lonely at the peak they say and it is very true. So what keeps you afloat in such a situation? When you have no help,but only stiff competition which wants to bring you down. It is your WHY. So, that's what I want to emphasize-that your soul needs to beconnected with your goals so that you can really keep going even in the toughest of the situations."

"Soul connected with goals... nice statement Jayant." Shekhar remarked.

KNOWING YOUR LIMITATIONS

A cool breeze motivated them to take a walk at the pool area.

"Let us take a walk." Jayant suggested.

"Yes, I need to exercise my legs or they will go numb", complained Shekhar rubbing his knees with his hands.

"The next step is to identify your limitations. Our goal setting has created a rosy picture till now, so this exercise will keep you grounded. Let us take the previous example where I wanted to double my net profit in six months. For that, I need to figure out what all needs to be done and what I can't do myself... Like visiting new markets,launching new products,need more funding, etc. At this stage, I have to identify, which areas are my strong suits, and which areas are my limitations?"

"Ok, you mean that I need to analyze myself also besides analyzing the market and economy?"

"Yes, let us say that you are good at product development or fundraising might be your core strength. Suppose you are not good at marketing or sales, then you need to write down these areas also where you are not good. This part will be called your limitation area."

This is a very important part of the process, but ignored most of the time... It's very important to find what all we can't do, but generally we don't define this and become the bottleneck in the entire process...

"Yea true, I never looked at this as what I am not good at; rather want to do everything myself, that's so powerful, I can see why I failed many times. Then, what to do next..."

"After writing down your limitations and your strengths you have to create an action plan, and align the team according to it."

MAKING LIST OF ACTIONS AND WHO WILL DO IT

"So, how do you make an action plan?" Shekhar asked. "Take my case; I want to increase my monthly profit to

100k USD in the next 6 months. So, what steps should my organization take in order to achieve this target? I will search for new profitable markets, I can do digital marketing or I can let my sales team to focus on those new markets where we want our business to grow. Maybe there are new ideas to capture the target market. Similarly, I need to focus on products/services which are more profitable. Some products might have low sales but higher profit margins. I need to identify them; or I might come up with a totally new product which will shoot up the profit immediately. Along with this, I have to manage finances also. I need to write down as to how much amount my company will need for which activity, how much funds I need to raise etc."

"Great and I was thinking that mere writing down goals was big enough…" Shekhar smiled.

"Your work doesn't stop here. You have to identify as to who will do these actions. I have seen many businesses fail because the owner thinks that he or she can do all these things. They even say that these are my goals; my staff has nothing to do with it. But when you ask them why they failed, they have no answer. Their team has no idea what is the goal of the organization. See, it is very important to align your organizational goals with each member of your team. Suppose you have made a plan for business development, then align your sales team or sales head with it. If there is a goal of fundraising then make sure your finance head is well aware of it. Assign them specific tasks and delegate your work especially in those areas which are your limitations."

"Ok, can I hire someone if I am not good in a particular area?"

"Yes, absolutely."

"What is your opinion about personal goals like health issues?" Shekhar asked reluctantly.

"Suppose you want to lose weight, then do you know what is the right diet or exercise for you?"

"No"Shekhar nodded.

"Then you need to hire a trainer, because that area is not your specialty. Only a trainer/dietician can guide you what to eat, how to exercise... besides that, you need to enroll your family members also, so that you can have an accountability partner at home who will keep a check on your eating habits. So, you see we create a team in such a way that everybody is aligned with our goals. This doubly ensures that we can achieve our goals."

"It also makes it a lot easier when you have so many people to support you"

"Absolutely." Jayant said.

11

SETTING MILESTONES

The evening was setting into night, but Shekhar was in no mood to leave the conversation. Jayant suggested that they could discuss further over drinks and dinner. They both agreed to meet at 8pm again.

"Tonight I will share the story of a dear friend who had gained a lot of weight and was getting married after six months. Everyone teased him for his heavy bridegroom avatar on his wedding day with his weight of 130 kg. He told me that he had enrolled in health centre, which had ensured him that they will make him lose 40 kg in six months. Then, he explained to me in detail what and how he had planned to lose weight."

"Did he lose weight?" Shekharwas anxious to know.

"No, when I went for his marriage function, he was coming in a car instead of mounting on a mare as is prevalent wedding custom in India. He had not lost even a single kg. That set me thinking that he had a specific goal, he had written and well planned his goal, he knew his deadline, he had even aligned his goals with his team of Health Centre, then what was the reason for his failure? What did he miss?"

Shekhar raised his shoulders, "What could have gone wrong?"

Jayant revealed, "When I asked my friend, he said that for the first two months, he kept on thinking that still there was a lot of time left, and after that his target of losing 40 kg started looking too big to achieve. The result was that he was never able to achieve his goal.

So what did he miss? Shekhar asked with concern.

"I think he should not have gone easy with himself." Shekhar said.

"Yes, self-discipline is important. But here the missing element is milestones. He didn't set up his milestones. He could have broken down his target of losing 40 kg into smaller goals like losing 7 kg per month. Losing 40 kg seems a big task, but breaking that in 7kg a month seems achievable and his brain would have accepted it. We need to break down our bigger goals into smaller ones, and the second most important thing is to follow result oriented activities."

"So, basically you mean to say that we should break down our goals into our daily activities and create a result oriented activity list to ensure that we are not distracted."

"True, let me elaborate it with an example from my life. My last year goal was to enroll 100 new clients in my business. That was my goal and not my team's goal. My team was doing its own stuff. So, it was my personal goal to add 100 new clients. We are into service industry and adding new clients is not a cakewalk. No matter in which industryyou are, you know how challenging it could be to bring 100 corporates on board in one year."

"So, what was your game plan?"

"I simply broke down my bigger goal into smaller goals. I realized that I earned 2-3 businesses through referrals every month,which made it to around 30 per year. Now, this is my organic growth for which I don't need to work much. For the remaining 70 clients, I calculated that if I meet 100 people, then I can convert 25 of them into business. So. this 25% is my conversion ratio. In this way, if I meet 24 prospects each month. then out of these, I can convert 6 into business. So, meeting 5 prospects became my one of weekly Result Oriented Activity (ROA). So you see from a big number of 100 people, I came down to small number-5 meetings per week. This will ultimately lead me to my target number."

"Great man!! and if you think about it...meeting 5 prospects every week doesn't seem to be an overwhelming task too."

"That is the importance of setting milestones and breaking down your bigger goals into smaller ones. Secondly, just keep on following your rules, never break them."

"But, where did you learn all this stuff ?" Shekhar asked inquisitively.

"I did a three month workshop just to understand setting milestones and organizing." Jayant revealed.

12

ORGANISING

"That's great, so you still find time for learning?"

"Yes, I invest in workshops and books. These are my success tools. The next important step is organizing yourself. Let us go back to our example of generating 100k USD in 6 months. Now you have defined your milestones; you know that in two months, you will reach 60k and 80k in 4 months, so that you reach your target of 100k in six months. Right?"

"Right, then you create your rules, your list your resultoriented activities which will take you to your goal…"

"But, if you miss to put them into your scheduler or calendar, then you can never possibly attain your goals…" Jayant completed the statement.

"Is that so?"

"Yes, Steve Jobs once said, "I can judge your future by looking at your calendar."That means he could predict anybody's future by just looking at his calendar. That is the power of a simple sounding calendar. So, if you are not organized, if your calendar is not packed, then you can see your days just passing by. You are not going to create big results in your life. There has not been any big businessman or any big leader, who has achieved big things, but is not organized or disciplined."

"I know about the calendar, but have not used it properly." Shekhar said, looking at his phone calendar.

"It is very important to create your own calendar. Technology has made things easier and your phone has in-built calendar and you can not only use them, but also set reminders for your daily asks or "Result Oriented Activities" (ROA). You can see how you can use it with optimization. It's very powerful. Once you start using it, you will wonder how you have been living without it till now. "So, I invite you to organize yourself and create your calendar based on your rules-which is your result-oriented activities."

It was 11 pm. Though Shekhar was in no mood to leave the conversation, but Jayant smiled and asked him to take some rest as they have enough time tomorrow.

13

TRACKING MECHANISM

The next morning both got up early for exercise. They decided to go for a brisk walk so that they could carry on with their conversation. After a long walk they sat down on a bench where Jayant pulled out his phone, he had tracking mechanism for his walk and exercise routine on his phone.

"I want that too, but somehow I don't walk or run regularly so I haven't installed it on my phone." Shekhar said, catching his breath.

"Tracking mechanisms are very important both for your health and for your goals."

"Tracking mechanism for goals? Is there an App for that too?"

"You can create your own tracking mechanism Shekhar.

That's again very important. You need to have your personal tracking mechanism. I call it—my compass. If you are not navigating yourself every day, then you are not going to generate results. I have my own tracking mechanism format which I studied during a workshop; on this, I write down all the tasks which I have to complete in order to achieve my goals."

"So, you update that on a daily basis?"

"Yes, every evening I tick down all the activities which I have completed. Initially, I was able to complete only 20-25% tasks listed in the mechanism. For many days, I was reluctant to take out my mechanism because I knew that I had not completed its activities, so one feels negative about it."

"So, how do you manage it?"

"Perseverance. Just keep on doing it every day till it becomes your habit and the brain can no longer give you excuses. Gradually I improved upon it and started completing my activities, because at the end of the day, I didn't want to experience that negative feeling."

"How to create this tracking mechanism?"

"Anybody can create their own tracking mechanism. All that you have to do is to write on a paper, the list of resultoriented activities which will help you in your growth, and take you closer to your goals. Prepare a list for the next thirty days. Every morning pull out that paper to check what activities are to be done today. This will keep you focused throughout the day. Next, what I did was I made my wife my accountability partner. She knows what I am supposed to do every day. Every evening she asks me what all have I done? What is missing and why is it missing? What I am going to do tomorrow so that it is not going to be missed."

"Who wants to be a failure in front of his wife...?" Shekhar said laughing.

"True, so I made extra efforts to complete my list so that I could look like a winner in front of her. This gave me a lot of positive reinforcement and helped me complete my tasks on time." Jayant winked.

"This tracking mechanism is a new concept."

"No, it has been followed on for many centuries but we have failed to notice it. How do you think the ships find their way in the ocean where there are no signposts? What will happen if the ship's captain doesn't keep an eye on compass and navigation? The ship will get lost in the ocean and never be able to reach its shore. Same way is your life—you won't even realize that you are missing your track. So, the tracking mechanism is very important and very powerful."

With this they again started running!!

14

MANIFESTATION

When they were coming down for breakfast, Shekhar pointed at the beautiful Ganesha idol in the hall, which they had not noticed earlier. Both Jayant and Shekhar folded their hands and bowed in front of the deity. When they sat for breakfast, Jayant saw that Shekhar was smiling.

"Why are you smiling like this?" Jayant asked.

"I thought that you were a non-believer. You know—' I believe in making my own destiny… I belong to that type of people."

"But I believe in the power of Almighty God or the universe as some people call it. In fact, I was going to tell you about the power of manifestation. How would you feel if you align your goals with the supreme power or the universe? What if God or a supernatural power is working to help you create your goals into reality? How would you feel if this happens?"

"I would feel extremely confident and totally sure of getting my things done. Who can doubt the power of the universe?"

"This is called the LAW of Attraction or manifestation process. I will give you a small but very powerful tool for manifestation. I know that your dream is to own an S-class, correct?"

"Yes bro, I love that car." Shekhar said getting excited like a kid.

"So you manifest it. Every morning for 15 minutes just close your eyes and think about it. Feel its leather seats, feel that your hands are at the steering wheel, feel the fragrance of the car. Now believe in your heart that it belongs to you. Picture yourself driving it, hit on the accelerator or imagine sitting at the backseat of this chauffeur driven S-class. You just have to be in that space for 15 minutes and let the universe work for you. Trust me it will create wonders in your life".

Similarly, use this process for all your goals!!

"You gave me a new statement bro—Aligning God with

Goals." Shekhar remarked.

15

CLOSURE

"I also need to emphasize on you Shekhar the importance of attending workshops and training sessions with your mentor or coach. You see, most of us know what to do and how to do, but we get distracted by life easily. No matter how hard our rules are; at one point or the other, we tend to deviate, or no longer feel like staying with our schedules. The coach or mentor is very crucial for hand-holding at such situations, where we are ready to sabotage our goal plans. So, I always keep on updating myself, sharpening my skills and mental strength through these workshops. Trust me, it is alife-long investment. It will transform your thought process and your life forever. That is my guarantee."

"I can see the transformation sitting in front of me. I think the reason for your tremendous growth is your bulletproof rules and these workshops."

"Absolutely, now, I want to quickly summarize what we have discussed so far, so that you can create your own goals according to it."

"Yes, please. I need to record that on a paper."

1. **Create crystal clear and SMART goals:** Specific, Measurable, Achievable, realistic, time- bound goals.

2. **Write down your goals:** Written words have power.

3. **Why you want to achieve your goals:** You have to make sure that you have the right reasons why you want to achieve these goals. Connect your soul with your goals.

4. **Identify your limitations:** You need to check your capabilities and research all possibilities.

5. **Make a list of result oriented activities:** Create an action plan of daily activities.

6. **Align your team with your goals:** You cannot be good at everything, hire experts wherever needed.

7. **Setting milestones:** Break down your goals into smaller tasks.

8. **Organizing:** Calendar management.

9. **Tracking mechanism:** Make your own navigation system; create an accountability partner to track your progress.

10. **Manifestation:** Align God with your Goals.

They quickly finished breakfast & went back to their room for the packing as they had to vacate the rooms...

Shekhar thanked Jayant as they went back to the car. "Ready to go back…?" Jayant asked Shekhar.

"…with new knowledge and a new power." came an enthusiastic reply from Shekhar.

"The power of goal setting, the power to create future" said

Jayant, pressing the accelerator.

CALL TO ACTION

Goal setting is a continuous process and "The Most" important skill to achieve anything and everything in life.

To further help you achieve amazing results and create a glorious life let's begin working together with Manuj as your mentor.

A valuable extension of the book, this Facebook page will provide the tools, information, and commentary you need to know about achieving goals...

Joi. our Community of Goal Achiever's at our FB page "Goal People"

9 789390 479603